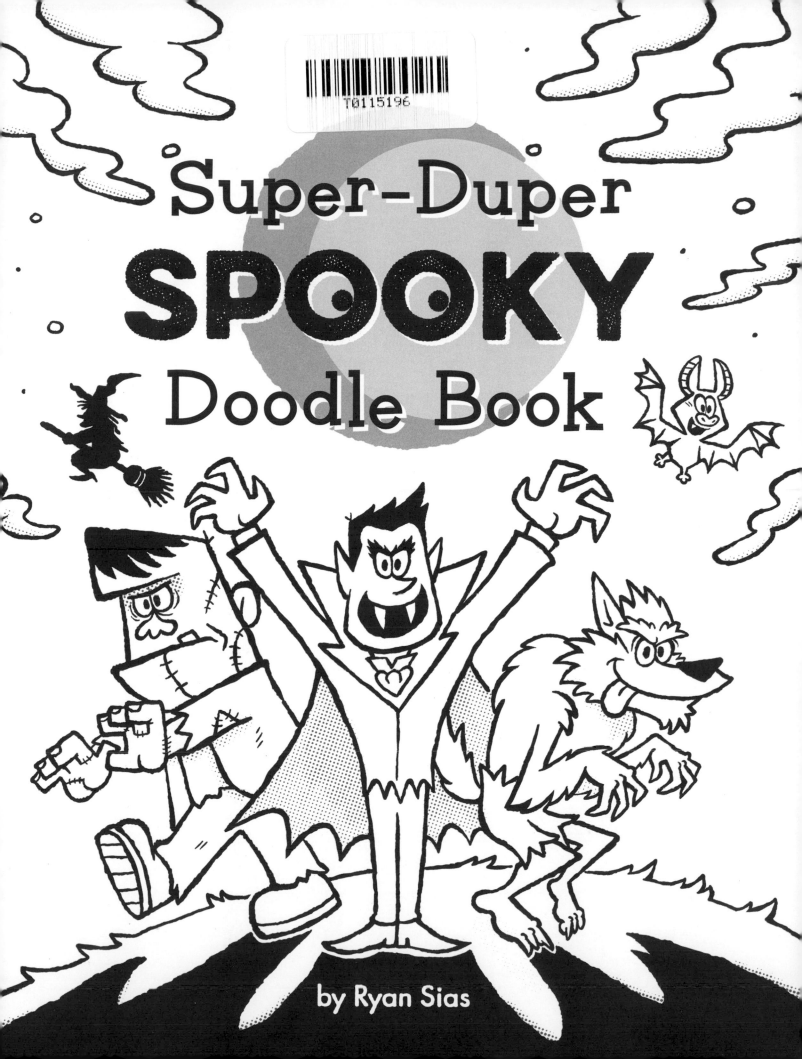

To my parents,

who allowed me to draw all the time

Text and illustrations copyright © 2018 by Ryan Sias

hmhco.com

The text of this book is set in Graham.
The display type was set in Plumbsky and Eveleth Dot.

ISBN: 978-1-328-81019-9

Manufactured in China
SCP 10 9 8 7 6 5 4 3 2 1
4500704597

Victor the Vampire

Draw your own.

Draw Victor the Vampire waking up in bed.

Give Victor a dramatic cape.

 **BONUS!** Draw bats flying around Victor.

Victor is about
to bite into his favorite
scary snack.
What could it be?
Draw it!

Story Starter

The dentist finds a cavity in one
of Victor's fangs. What happens next?
Write a story!

9

Brody the Bat

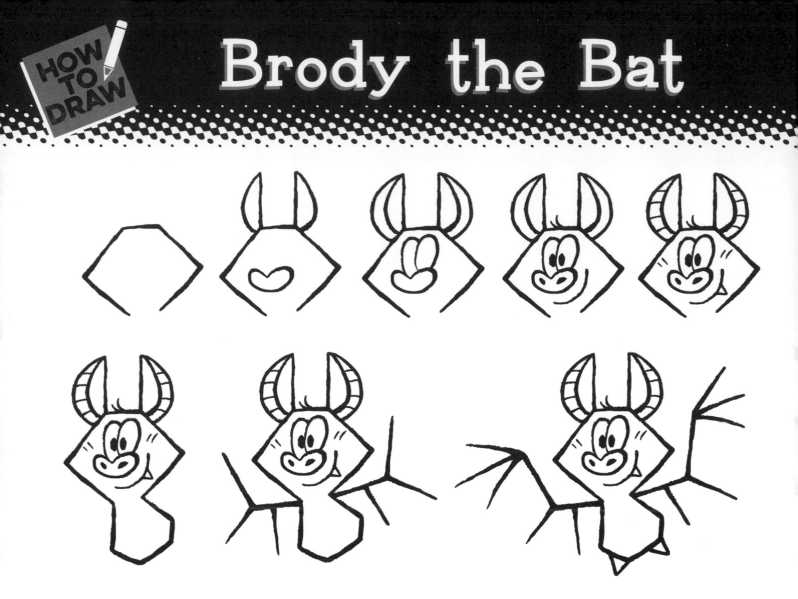

Draw your own.

Brody the Bat likes to sleep
upside down in murky caves.
Draw Brody sleeping next
to his friends.

Brody is flying and finds
a horrible monster has
hatched out of an egg.
Draw the horrible monster!

Find and Color the Hidden Items

ghost · witch hat · coffin · pear · candle · wishbone · moon · cat · pencil

Zoey the Zombie

Draw your own.

Zoey the Zombie loves chasing people. Draw her running after them!

You can make anyone into a zombie—
it's eerily easy. Here's how:

1. Draw a person.

2. Draw circles and lines around the eyes. Add drool.

3. Draw ripped clothing and wild hair.

4. Add bite marks.

Draw your own.

The zombies are
multiplying!
Zombify this family.

Zoey cannot find her usual meal of brains. Draw something else she can eat.

Story Starter

Zoey has wandered into a
beauty salon, looking for brains!
What happens?

19

Wanda the Witch

Draw your own.

Wanda loves making
wicked potions.
Draw Wanda
stirring her kettle.

Wanda has a spooktacular
witch's hat. Draw it.

22

Wanda needs some ghastly
ingredients for her spell.
Fill the glass jars with
ingredients like frog warts,
eyeballs, and hair of troll.

Wanda's magic crystal ball shows things that cause a fright!

Draw something frightening in her crystal ball.

BONUS! Draw lots of warts on Wanda's face.

Claudia the Black Cat

Draw your own.

Put Claudia on the front of Wanda's broom.

Claudia is about to pounce on a gruesome animal for Wanda's witch's brew! Draw it.

Claudia has broken Wanda's magic mirror! What happens next? Tell the story.

HOW TO DRAW

Draw your own.

Terry and his friends
are terrifying the city.
Draw them on the buildings.

31

Terry has caught something unusual in his web.
What did he catch? Draw it.

People are running
away from Terry.
Draw them.

····· |BONUS!| How to Draw Small People ·······

Terry sees something strange
when he looks in the window.
What is it?

34

Story Starter

Terry sees animals in cages
at the zoo. What does he do?
Tell the story.

Maya the Mummy

Draw your own.

Maya loves making tomb raiders shriek.
Draw Maya scaring the tomb raiders.

Help Maya redecorate her sarcophagus.

BONUS! Fill the room with expensive artifacts like gold, fancy jewelry, and silver vases.

Draw Maya's mummy mommy.

Maya is reading
an ancient scroll.
What is written on it?

BONUS! Draw beetles on the wall and the scroll.

Find and Color the Hidden Items

Draw your own.

Frank's alive!
Draw Frank N. Stein
being brought to life.

Frank is lonely.
Create a pet for him that
is part dog, part cat,
and part bird.

Frank wants a family.
Create them!

Story Starter

What happens when Frank 'n' family go to the beach? Tell a silly story.

Draw your own.

AHOOOOOO!
Draw Wayne howling
at the moon.

BONUS! Add bats in the sky.

Wayne finds another person who's changing into a werewolf. Draw it!

BONUS! Give him lots of hair!

Give Wayne big teeth!

BONUS! Also give him sharp claws.

Grik the Goblin

Draw your own.

Grik gobbles candy. Draw Grik grabbing candy from the trick-or-treaters.

Draw all the candy
that Grik grabbed.

BONUS! Add something Grik WOULDN'T want to eat.

Story Starter

Grik wants to grab candy from the werewolf and decides to play a trick on him. What trick does Grik play? Tell the story.

Gus the Ghost

Draw your own.

Gus gets ghostly delight from haunting the farm. Draw Gus.

Gus likes to scare pigs and chickens, Draw a pig or chicken getting scared by Gus.

Find and Color the Hidden Items

crow
bone
pot
moon
tombstone
rabbit
glove
key
boot

Ned and Nikki

Draw your own.

Monsters are everywhere.
Draw Ned and Nikki
hiding from them.

Ned and Nikki have made it safely home.
But something is in the closet!
Draw an animal zombie in there!

Ned hears something bump under his bed. Draw something creepy under the bed.

UFOs and Allen the Alien

Draw your own.

The UFO invasion has begun!
Draw lots of UFOs.

The UFO has landed!
Draw what comes
out of it.

BONUS! Draw the people's reactions to seeing Allen the Alien.

An alien has landed in your backyard. What do you say to it? Tell the story.

Find and Color the Hidden Items

belt

tooth

crown

hammer

arrow

torch

horn

mug

69

Henrik the Hydra

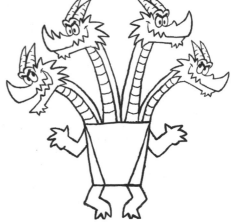

Draw your own.

Draw Henrik flying
up to the troll castle.

Henrik scares away the guard
trolls with his fire breath.
Draw it.

Henrik breaks a hole in the castle wall and discovers a troll warrior guarding treasure. Draw the troll.

BONUS! Draw the treasure also!

Tasso the Troll

Draw your own.

Tasso is a terrifying cook.
Draw Tasso cooking.

BONUS! Put toenails and spiders on the frying pans.

Tasso makes his specialty—spaghetti and eyeballs!
Draw the eyeballs.

BONUS! Add bugs and worms to the spaghetti.

Fill the sock burrito with Tasso's favorite slimy stuffing ingredients.

Story Starter

Tasso loves making ghastly meals.
How does Tasso get his gross
ingredients? Tell the story.

Draw your own.

Draw Slimy under the fishing boat.

Draw the toxic garbage
Slimy smells.

carrot
lightning bolt
fish
apple core
turtle
snake
skull
eyeball
finger

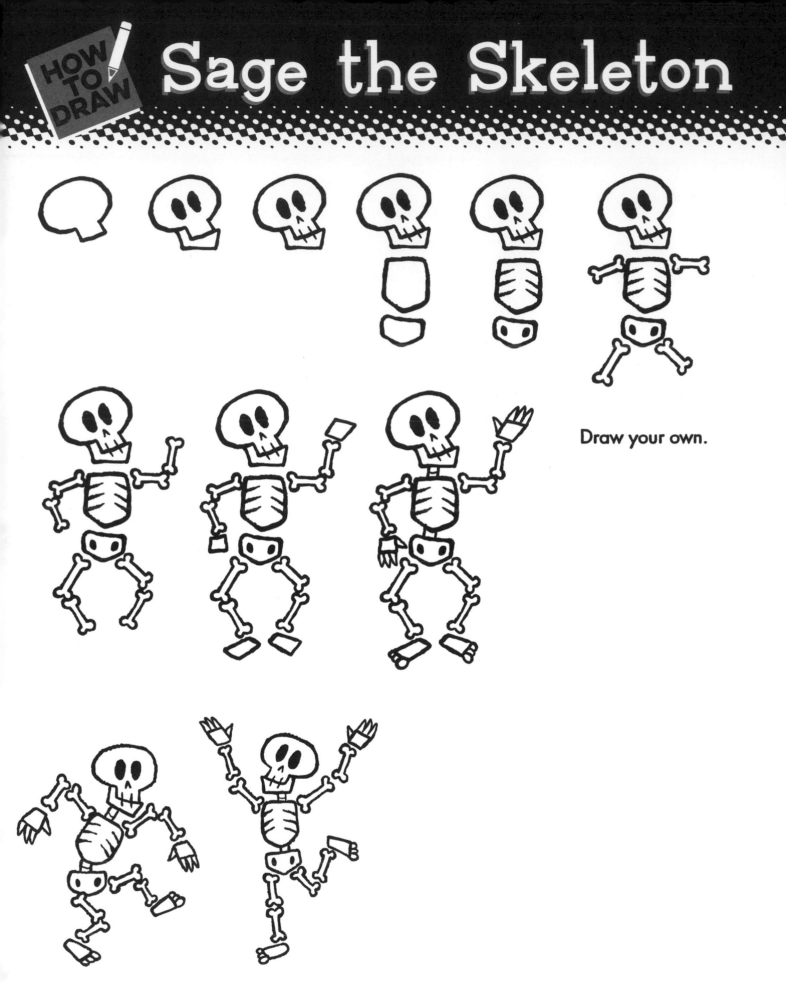

Draw your own.

Sage loves rocking out with the Band of Bones! Draw Sage and her friends dancing.

Give this skeleton a more bonetastic drum set so he can rock louder!

BONUS! Draw skulls on the drums.

Oh no! Sage's head fell off while she was dancing. What could she use as a new head?

It's Victor the Vampire's 190th surprise birthday party! Tasso has made a creepy cake for the party. Decorate it!

All the monsters are bringing ghastly gifts for Victor. Create a pile of gifts for him.

BONUS! Add balloons that look like eyeballs.

Shhh . . . Victor is coming!
Everyone hide!
Draw something for
Claudia the Cat to hide behind.

Surprise!
Happy birthday,
Victor!

Draw a ghost jumping
out from behind
the tombstone to
surprise Victor.

92 **BONUS!** Add some jack-o-lanterns.

How does Victor react
to the surprise?
Draw his reaction.

BONUS! Add bats flying around him.

It's a frightful dance fest!
Draw some funny dancing
legs on Max the Mummy.

BONUS! Add confetti.

This party is going all night!
Give everyone strange
and spooky party hats.

You did a DE-FRIGHTFUL job drawing and doodling!

Did you spot all the moons?
Color the ones you found.

Have a spooktacular evening!

And don't forget to sticker!

p. 13

3 7 12 15 21

28 49 50 51 53

54 57 58 59 61

65 66 69 71 89

p. 25

p. 41

p. 46

p. 59

p. 69

p. 78

p. 83

p. 88